THE ANCIENT MARINER

THE PLAY OF
The Ancient Mariner

DRAMATISED BY MICHAEL BOGDANOV
FROM THE POEM BY S.T. COLERIDGE

HEINEMANN

Heinemann Educational Books Ltd,
Halley Court, Jordan Hill, Oxford OX2 8EJ

OXFORD   LONDON   EDINBURGH   MELBOURNE
SYDNEY   AUCKLAND   IBADAN   NAIROBI   GABORONE
HARARE   KINGSTON   PORTSMOUTH NH (USA)
SINGAPORE   MADRID

ISBN 0 435 23081 6

Cover design by Richard Bird

Printed in Great Britain by
J. W. Arrowsmith Ltd, Bristol

THE RIME OF THE ANCIENT MARINER

Samuel Taylor Coleridge

The Idea of the Poem

An Extract from the Diary of William Wordsworth

In the Autumn of 1797 he [Coleridge], my sister and myself started from Alfoxden pretty late in the afternoon with a view to visit Linton and the Valley of Stones near to it, as our united funds were very small we agreed to defray the expense of the tour by writing a poem to be sent to the *New Monthly Magazine*. Accordingly, we set off and proceeded along the Quantock Hills towards Watchet; in the course of this walk was planned the poem of the 'Ancient Mariner', founded on a dream, as Mr Coleridge said of his friend Mr Cruickshank. Much of the greatest part of the story was Mr Coleridge's invention, but certain parts I suggested; for example, some crime was to be committed which should bring upon the Old Navigator, as Coleridge was afterwards delighted to call him, the spectral persecution as a consequence of that crime and his own wanderings. I had been reading in Shelvock's *Voyages* a day or two before, that while doubling Cape Horn, they frequently saw albatrosses in that latitude . . . 'Suppose', said I, 'you represent him as having killed one of these birds on entering the South Sea and that the spirits of these regions take upon them to avenge the crime.' The incident was thought fit for the purpose and adopted accordingly. I also suggested the navigation of the ship by dead men, but do not recollect that I had anything more to do with the scheme of the poem. We began the composition on that, to me, memorable evening. As we endeavored to proceed cojointly our respective manners proved so widely different that it would have been quite presumptious in me to do anything but separate from an undertaking upon which I could only have been a clog . . . 'The Ancient Mariner' grew and grew till it became too important for our first object, which was limited to our expectation of five pounds; we began to think of a volume which was to consist, as Mr Coleridge has told the world, of poems chiefly on supernatural subjects, taken from common life, but looked at, as much as might be, through an imaginative medium.

INTRODUCTION AND NOTES ON PRODUCTION

Michael Bogdanov

What follows is an interpretation of Samuel Taylor Coleridge's poem for stage. Since it was originally conceived for an audience of 6–12 year-olds, certain aspects are ignored and others amplified. The production concentrates on the narrative and attempts to support the text with dramatic, visual and audial images.

The wedding acts as a framework for the show at all times. When returning to the present there must be music and dancing taking place around the boat, performed with a ghostly quality.

The ship is created with rigging, mast, ropes and sail. All can be rigged during the course of the action and the mariners can climb, pull, point and haul whenever the text demands. The sail acts as a backcloth to project images and lighting effects. Folk dance and shanties are used to provide background atmosphere and the use of a highly imaginative sound tape is most important. Since it is physically a very demanding show, the company must take great care in rope climbing, swinging, etc. It can be performed with as few as nine people or as many as you like. The ideal is to have one group to perform the mariners and one to provide the 'off-boat' effects – voices, dancing, ribbon-whirling, etc. The set should have several levels – not only to create a more realistic area for the boat but to create a division for the 'off-boat' world. The show works best in a thrust-stage situation, with mariners able to climb out over the audience, but the visual side is effective in any space.

The 'floating in the air' around the boat may be created in various ways e.g. flying, a fork-lift truck, T.V. camera dollies (i.e moving arms mounted on a mobile frame), lasers, or simply with free-standing towers and ladders. Whatever system is used, the air around the boat is important and some means must be found of creating the effects.

The costumes can be from any period, the poem and the play are timeless.

One final note. The Ancient Mariner uses a radio-microphone round his neck. This is to enable him to be heard at all times, above the music and sound effects. Without this, realistic levels cannot be achieved and some other way must be found to create the atmosphere.

The Albatross

'Albatross' is the name for more than a dozen species of seabird, large, gentle and friendly creatures.

The most impressive of them is the Wandering Albatross of the southern seas. It is an enormous snow-white bird with jet black wing tips, a long beak that hooks downwards at the tip and webbed feet like a duck. It is the largest of all seabirds. It weighs seven to twelve kilos and its wing span can be up to three metres. The bird travels alone and is capable of following a ship for days without resting on the water. At intervals it glides down to feed on refuse from the ship and on squid and shrimp churned up by the ship's wake.

The albatross spends the majority of its life at sea and comes to the land only to breed.

It is the most spectacular of gliders and can stay aloft for hours in windy weather without ever flapping its huge wings, wheeling almost without effort. It is a monarch of the ocean skies and has no equal in long-distance flight over the deep salt waters of the world. An albatross can cruise hundreds of miles in a single day.

The albatross is an ancient bird. Fossils of ten species have been found in rocks. Some lived 50 million years ago. Much of the early information about these birds came from observations by uneducated and often superstitious men on whaling ships. Shipboard stories passed from man to man and from generation to generation. The sailor folklore was cleverly written into tales of the sea and became legends. In the mind of many readers stories such as 'The Rime of the Ancient Mariner' became fact.

In the days of sail an albatross flying round a ship in mid ocean was an omen of wind and bad weather to come. It was very unlucky to kill it because, like the sea-gull and the stormy petrel, it was thought to embody the restless soul of some dead mariner. This belief was once very widespread amongst deep-water sailors and probably helped to preserve these magnificent birds in the southern ocean; but evidently it was not quite universal for it was not unknown for the less superstitious to shoot an albatross to make tobacco pouches from its webbed feet or to take one on a baited hook for meat. Pipes were made from their hollow wing bones, hand muffs from their breasts and even huge cups from their beaks. They were also slaughtered in large numbers for their feathers, used as swansdown in the millinery trade.

Sea Shanties

A shanty is the name given to a rousing and tuneful song sung by sailors at work in the days of sailing ships.

On sailing day the cry would go up 'Man the capstan' and the crew would crowd round this cylindrical object on the foredeck, take the capstan bars from the nearby rack, ship them in the holes at the top of the capstan, and start to turn it by pushing on the bars. The anchor chain would slowly be hove in as the capstan revolved while the men stamped steadily round it. These men would sing a chorus to verses sung (frequently improvised) by a member of the crew called a shantyman. He was a person of importance on the ship, being excused all hauling and heaving work, and merely stood near his working mates to sing shanty verses. He would often first sing the chorus of the particular shanty chosen for the one job, to remind the men which one it was to be.

The origin of the word 'shanty' has been explained in various ways:
1. that it derives from the French word 'chanter' meaning to sing;
2. that it comes from the old English word 'chant' or 'chaunt';
3. that it comes from the drinking dens of the ports of the Gulf of Mexico where seamen gathered, called shanties;
4. that it comes from the huts, or shanties, inhabited by West Indian negroes: when the owner of one of these huts wished to move house he did so simply by hauling on ropes and moving it bodily on rollers. While this work was in progress those hauling would sing choruses to verses improvised by a man on top of the hut – known in fact as the shantyman.

Early shanties consisted of little more than wild cries that accompanied work, rather like the shouting of 'Left, Right' to encourage marching men to keep time and to keep going. Some of the earlier tunes are undoubtedly derived from the tunes played at capstan and halliards by fiddlers in the Royal Navy ships.

The greatest period for the shanty was from the middle of the nineteenth century until about 1880. Although after this date they were freely used, the jobs at which they accompanied began to alter. However, they continued to stimulate effort and provide entertainment until the singing of them in working conditions died out with the last of the long-distance sailing ships.

Hewlett

This Irish tune is traditionally attributed to the most famous of all Irish harpers Carolan (1670–1738). It is of the type known as a *planxty*, usually a tune made in honour of a patron and not necessarily bound to the even structure of dance music.

The tune is used for the wedding dance for the bride on page 1 and should be jaunty but not too fast.

Props List

12 large white handkerchiefs
6 sets of Morris bells with green, yellow & red ribbons
Crossbow – to fire, but without bolt
Turning capstan + 6 removable rods to turn it
Flying Albatross rod puppet
Dead Albatross to be hung round the Young Mariner's neck
Wooden cross on breakable chain – Young Mariner
Wooden cup with 2 dice (or substitute – not seen)
2 white ribbons – 2.5m × 25cm
1 blue ribbon – 2.5m × 25cm
1 green ribbon – 2.5m × 25cm
1 black ribbon – 2.5m × 25cm
4 red ribbons – 2.5m × 25cm
Flute
Flagolet in 'C'
3 Flagolets in 'D'
Mandolin
Concertina
Bodrhan (drum) and two headed stick
1 pair made-up 'bones'
Ship's bell – practical
5 sheath knives
3 pairs gloves – for Mariners to climb with if necessary
Tambourine
Confetti
(Musical instruments and knives could be personal)

Sound

(Not necessarily in order and only suggestions from original production.)

Pre-show accordion music (recorded or live)
Music – accordion – for wedding – fade
Wing building to storm
Thunder crack
Strong wind
Whine
Ice cracking – continuous
Large ice crack
Breeze in the ship's rigging
Albatross sound
Crack of cross-bow and sound of dying Albatross
Hornpipe
Sea as boat speeds through it
Creaking of timbers
Whine in ghost ship sound
Three whistles (ear shattering)
Death and souls leaving sound
Water snakes sound
Rain
Wind getting closer
Ship being tossed around
Reverb. for antiphonal sounds
Reverb. for voices in air
Breeze
Celestial choir
Ship's warning bell
Rowing boat
Rumbling building to thunder crack as boat goes down
Morris dance with live or recorded music
NB: radio microphone for Ancient Mariner
      reverb.
      microphone for offstage

Some Background Sources to Help with Research

The Rime of the Ancient Mariner, S.T. Coleridge, illus. Gustave Dore, Dover, 1970

The Annotated Ancient Mariner, S.T. Coleridge: notes M. Gardner, New American Library, 1974

A Preface to Coleridge, Allan Grant, Longman, 1972

Coleridge: Writers & Their Backgrounds, Ed. R.L. Brett, G. Bell & Sons, 1971

Sea Serpents, Sailors & Sceptics, Graham J. McEwan, Routledge & Kegan Paul, 1978

Strange Mysteries of the Sea, Len Ortzen, Arthur Baker, 1976

The Amazing World of the Sea, Jennifer Cochrane, Angus & Robertson, 1976

Sea Shanties, Stan Hugil, Barrie & Jenkins Ltd, 1977

Songs Under Sail, Peter Heaton & Maria Bird, Burke, 1963

Wonders of the World of the Albatross, Harvey & Mildred Fisher, Windmill Press, 1976

How Birds Live, Robert Burton, Elsevier-Phaidon, 1975

Without A Trace, Charles Berlitz, Souvenir Press, 1977

The Bermuda Triangle: Mystery Solved, Lawrence D. Kusche, New English Library, 1975

The Great Age of Sail, Ed. Joseph Jobe, Patrick Stephens Ltd, 1967

Historic Ships of the World, William C. Heine, David & Charles, 1977

The Encyclopedia Britannica

THE CHARACTERS

Ancient Mariner
Wedding-Guest
Young Mariner
Woman
Death
Voices
Pilot
Hermit
Boy
Bride
Wedding-Guests
Mariners

The Ancient Mariner was first performed at the Young Vic, Christmas 1979. This version was performed at the National Theatre, Christmas 1984, with the following cast:

The Ancient Mariner	Michael Bryant
The Bride/Death	Jessica Turner
Mariner/Wedding-Guest/Boy	Robin Chandler
Mariner/Pilot	Charles Baillie
Mariner/Voice	Robert Ralph
Mariner/Hermit	Robin Lloyd
Mariner	William Sleigh
The Young Mariner	Frederick Warder
Mariner/Groom	Paul Bentall

Director	Michael Bogdanov
Designer	Marty Flood

PART ONE

As the audience arrives there is traditional music, singing and dancing outside the theatre and in the foyer. This is the wedding celebration. The foyer may be decked out specially. The stage is also hung with bunting and flags disguising the framework of a boat which at this point should look like the quay-side, with coiled ropes, lobster-pots, nets etc. The houselights are dim. The festivities continue into the auditorium. As the houselights go the music fades and the ANCIENT MARINER *comes slowly into a spot.*

ANCIENT MARINER:
    I pass like night from land to land,
    I have strange power of speech
    The moment that his face I see
    I know the man that must hear me
    To him my tale I teach.

The COMPANY, *as wedding-guests burst on to the stage and lift the* BRIDE *up on to the capstan, throwing confetti over her. They all have instruments and immediately they strike up a solo wedding dance for the bride. The tune is 'Hewlett'. At end, they freeze.*

ANCIENT MARINER:
    The moment that his face I see
    I know the man that must hear me
    To him my tale I teach.

The WEDDING-GUESTS *unfreeze and stream off past the* ANCIENT MARINER . *The music is taken up on tape or continues live. The* ANCIENT MARINER *stops the last* WEDDING-GUEST *with outstretched hand.*

1

WEDDING-GUEST:
> By thy long grey beard and glittering eye
> Now wherefore stopp'st thou me?
> The Bridegroom's doors are opened wide,
> And I am next of kin;
> The guests are met, the feast is set:
> May'st hear the merry din.

Up stage the BRIDE *is lifted high in the air and taken off.*

ANCIENT MARINER:
> There was a ship –

WEDDING-GUEST:
> Hold off! Unhand me, grey-beard loon!

ANCIENT MARINER:
> There was a ship –

Immediately lights up. Shanty. The MARINERS *rush on. (These are former* WEDDING-GUESTS, *now changed.) The boat is rigged from scratch – hauling up the ropes, sails etc. A method must be found to haul the rigging from the ground and secure it safely so that the* MARINERS *can climb it. When it is complete the crew settle down to man the boat.*

The shanty 'Heave away me Johnny' can have as many verses as necessary and can be made up by the cast. It is to cover the rigging of the boat, which should look spectacular.

HEAVE AWAY ME JOHNNY

> Oh there's some that's bound for New York town
> And some that's bound for France.

CHORUS:
> Heave away me Johnny. Heave away.

2

And there's some that's bound for the Bengal Bay
To teach them whales a dance.
CHORUS:
Heave away me Johnny boy. We're all bound to go.

Our pilot he's awaiting for the turning of the tide,
CHORUS
And then me girls we'll be gone again
On the good and westerly wind.
CHORUS

So farewell to you me Kingston girls,
Farewell St. Andrew's dock.
CHORUS
If ever we return again we'll
Make your cradles rock.
CHORUS

So come all of you hard weather sailing men
That round the cape of storms
CHORUS
And be sure your boots and your oilskins on
Or you'll wish you'd never been born.
CHORUS

Crew indicate passing of land etc. The ANCIENT
MARINER *holds his position centre for narration.*
Throughout the action he will only shift his position
occasionally. The capstan is his natural resting point.

ANCIENT MARINER:
The ship was cheered, the harbor cleared.

The MARINERS *watch land pass. Projections on the sail.*

Merrily did we drop
Below the kirk, below the hill
Below the light house top.

The shanty continues for a couple of verses hummed.
MARINERS *busy themselves in activity.*

ANCIENT MARINER:
>The Sun came up upon the left,
>Out of the sea came he!
>And he shone bright, and on the right
>Went down into the sea.

*Lighting indicates a slow build to full for the burning
sun. Action slows down. A slow shanty starts,
'Lowlands Away' with whistle accompaniment.*

LOWLANDS AWAY

>I dreamed a dream the other night
>Lowlands, lowlands away me boys
>I dreamed a dream the other night
>Lowlands away me John.

>I dreamed I saw me own true love
>Lowlands, lowlands away me boys
>I dreamed I saw me own true love
>Lowlands away me John.

>I dreamed me love was drowned and dead
>Lowlands, lowlands away me boys
>I dreamed me love was drowned and dead
>Lowlands away me John.

ANCIENT MARINER:
>Higher and higher every day,
>Till over the mast at noon –

Shanty finishes. Wind is heard. MARINERS *start to trim
ropes and sail. Storm builds, louder and louder. The
lights dip up and down. Sudden burst of thunder and
lightning flash.*

ANCIENT MARINER:

And now the storm-blast came and he
Was tyrannous and strong:
He struck with his o'ertaking wings,
And chased us south along.

Sound continues through. The MARINERS *climb, pull, rig, hang, are thrown around etc.*

With sloping masts and dipping prow,
As who pursued with yell and blow
Still treads the shadow of his foe,
And forward bends his head,
The ship drove fast, loud roared the blast,
And southward aye we fled,

The sounds gradually fade. The boat is brought under control. Lights change. Mist, snow effects. A strange sound is heard.

And now there came both mist and snow,
And it grew wondrous cold:
And ice, mast-high, came floating by,
As green as emerald,

Shapes of ice are seen on the sails.

And through the drifts the snowy cliffs
Did send a dismal sheen:
Nor shapes of men nor beasts we ken –
The ice was all between.

Cracking sounds continue through the whole sequence.

The ice was here, the ice was there,
The ice was all around:
It crackled and growled, and roared and howled,
Like noises in a swound!

The Albatross appears up stage as if floating in space, created by the rod puppet method or by separate albatrosses that cross the stage left to right and back again on pre-strung flying wires.

> At length did cross an Albatross
> Through the fog it came;
> As if it had been a Christian soul,
> We hailed it in God's name.

The Albatross is moved slowly around.

ANCIENT MARINER:
> It ate the food it ne'er had eat,
> And round and round it flew.

Rending of sail. Loud crack.

> The ice did split with a thunder-fit;
> The helmsman steered us through!

The MARINERS *cheer and man the boat.*

> And a good south wind sprang up behind;
> And Albatross did follow,
> And every day, for food or play,
> Came to the mariners' hollo!

MARINERS *haul ropes and sing shanty 'Way Haul Away'. At finish the* MARINERS *hum and lights change to night.*

WAY HAUL AWAY

Talk about you sailor girls around the corner Sally,

CHORUS:
> Way haul away we'll haul away the bowline,
> Way haul away we'll haul away Joe
> But you wouldn't go to tea with the girls from
>   Bootle Alley

CHORUS:
Way haul away we'll haul away the bowline,
Way haul away we'll haul away Joe.

When I was just a little kid me mother she told me,
If I didn't kiss the girls me lips would all go mouldy.
CHORUS
King Louis was the king of France before the
 revolution,
But the people chopped his head off and it spoilt his
 constitution.
CHORUS
Well I thought I heard the old man say it's time to
 hit the road and go,
But when I get back to Liverpool you pretty girls
 are going to know.

ANCIENT MARINER:
In mist or cloud, on mast or shroud,
It perched for vespers nine;
Whiles all the night, through fog-smoke white,
Glimmered the white moon-shine.

*Cut back to the present with music, bride and dancers
up stage. They perform a ghostly half-time dance
around the ship. The other images freeze, The*
WEDDING-GUEST *appears at* ANCIENT MARINER'S
side.

WEDDING-GUEST:
God save thee, ancient Mariner!
From the fiends, that plague thee thus! –
Why look'st thou so?

ANCIENT MARINER:
                              With my cross bow
I shot the Albatross.

YOUNG MARINER – *steps forward into spot at shoulder
of* ANCIENT MARINER, *with arrowless crossbow and*

7

shoots Albatross. A strange sound is heard as the Albatross floats slowly to the ground. They turn to look at the YOUNG MARINER.

YOUNG MARINER:
> With my crossbow
> I shot the Albatross.

Sits on capstan, whistles and polishes bow. MARINERS *gradually go back to work.*

ANCIENT MARINER:
> The Sun now rose upon the right:
> Out of the sea came he,
> Still hid in mist, and on the left
> Went down into the sea.
>
> And the good south wind still blew behind,
> But no sweet bird did follow.
> Nor any day for food or play
> Came to the mariners' hollo!

SAILOR 1:
> You have done a hellish thing,
> And it will work us woe.

Dead Albatross is brought forward and lain on the ground. This is a real, much larger, bird than the one used to create the flying.

SAILOR 2:
> O Mariner, you have killed the bird
> That makes the breeze to blow.

SAILOR 3:
> Ah wretch! This day the bird to slay
> That makes the breeze to blow!

The sun rises in a blaze.

ANCIENT MARINER:
  Nor dim nor red, like God's own head,
  The glorious Sun uprist:
  Then all averred

SAILOR 4:
  You have killed the bird
  That brought the fog and mist.

SAILOR 5:
  'Twas right, that day, such birds to slay,
  That bring the fog and mist.

The SAILORS *celebrate with a hornpipe and a dance
played on whistle and drum. The tune is 'Londonderry'.*

YOUNG MARINER:
  The fair breeze blew, the white foam flew,
  The furrow followed free;
  We were the first that ever burst
  Into that silent sea.

The MARINERS *busy themselves, then gradually slow
to a halt.*

ANCIENT MARINER:
  Down dropt the breeze, the sails dropt down,
  'Twas sad as sad could be;
  And we did speak only to break

YOUNG MARINER:
  The silence of the sea!

Plaintive pipe music. The MARINERS *stretch out.*

YOUNG MARINER:
  All in a hot and copper sky,
  The bloody Sun, at noon,
  Right up above the mast did stand,
  No bigger than the Moon.

Strange sound of boards creaking and high pitched whine.

ANCIENT MARINER:
> Day after day, day after day,
> We've stuck, nor breath nor motion;
> As idle as a painted ship
> Upon a painted ocean.
>
> Water, water, everywhere,
> And all the boards did shrink;

SAILOR 4:
> Water, water, everywhere,
> Nor any drop to drink.

ANCIENT MARINER:
> The very deep did rot:

SAILOR 1:
>   Oh Christ!
> That ever this should be!

SAILOR 2:
> Yea, slimy things do crawl with legs
> Upon the slimy sea,

Night and dancing lights.

ANCIENT MARINER:
> About, about, in reel and rout
> The death-fires danced at night;
> The water, like a witch's oils,
> Burned green, and blue and white.

Long silk ribbons snake in and out of a colour wheel, whirled by two members of the Company.

> And some in dreams assuréd were
> Of the spirit that plagued us so;

SAILOR 1:

 Nine fathom deep he has followed us
 From the land of mist and snow.

ANCIENT MARINER:

 And every tongue, through utter drought,
 Is withered at the root;

SAILOR 3:

 I cannot speak, nor more than if
 I had been choked with soot.

The MARINERS *begin to look at the* YOUNG MARINER.
They climb down and grab him, draw him up on to a
net where he hangs suspended.

YOUNG MARINER:

 Ah! well-a-day! What evil looks
 Had I from old and young!
 Instead of the cross, the Albatross
 About my neck was hung.

The cross is ripped from his neck and the huge
Albatross suspended.

Sounds of boards creaking still.

ANCIENT MARINER:

 There passed a weary time. Each throat
 Was parched, and glazed each eye.

The lights start to change to a blood red sunset. YOUNG
MARINER *is left hanging from the rigging.*

SAILOR 2:

 A weary time! A weary time!

ANCIENT MARINER:

 How glazed each weary eye
 When looking westward, I beheld

11

YOUNG MARINER:
   A something in the sky.

ANCIENT MARINER:
   At first it seemed –

   A strange sound is heard.

SAILOR 3:
                  A little speck,

ANCIENT MARINER:
   And then it seemed

SAILOR 5:
                  A mist;

SAILOR 4:
   It moves, it moves,

ANCIENT MARINER:
                  And took at last
   A certain shape

YOUNG MARINER:
                  I wist.

SAILOR 1:
   A speck,

SAILOR 2:
            A mist,

SAILOR 3:
                  A shape

YOUNG MARINER:
                        I wist!

   And still it neared and neared:
   As if it dodged a water-sprite,
   It plunged and tacked and veered,

12

With throats unslaked, with black lips baked,
We could not laugh or wail;
Through utter drought all dumb we stood!
I bit my arm, I sucked the blood
And cried

YOUNG MARINER:
>   A sail! A sail!

ANCIENT MARINER:
> With throats unslaked, with black lips baked,
> Agape they heard me call:

ANCIENT MARINER:
> Gramercy! they for joy did grin,
> And all at once their breath drew in,
> As they were drinking all.

SAILOR 4:
> See! See! She tacks no more!
> Hither to work us weal;

SAILOR 5:
> Without a breeze, without a tide,
> She steadies with upright keel!

ANCIENT MARINER:
> The western wave was all a-flame.
> The day was well nigh done!
> Almost upon the western wave
> Rested the broad bright Sun;

YOUNG MARINER:
> When that strange shape drove suddenly
> Betwixt us and the Sun.

Back light. Shadow of strange rib-shape boat is seen on the sail.

ANCIENT MARINER:

> And straight the Sun was flecked with bars,

SAILOR 3:

> Heaven's Mother send us grace!

ANCIENT MARINER:

> As if through a dungeon-grate he peered
> With broad and burning face.

YOUNG MARINER:

> Alas!

ANCIENT MARINER:

> Thought I, and my heart beat loud

YOUNG MARINER:

> How fast she nears and nears!

SAILOR 2:

> Are those her sails that glance in the Sun
> Like restless gossameres?

SAILOR 5:

> Are those her ribs through which the Sun
> Doth peer, as through a grate?

SAILOR 4:

> And is that Woman all her crew?

SAILOR 3:

> Is that a Death?

SAILOR 2:

> And are there two?

SAILOR 1:

> Is Death that Woman's mate?

From back slowly comes the Death boat. It is a skeletal boat with a ribbed mast with scraps of tattered sail. DEATH *is a skull in black and the* WOMAN *is in white.*

SAILOR 4:
    Her lips are red,

SAILOR 3:
                  Her looks are free,

SAILOR 1:
    Her locks are yellow as gold:

SAILOR 2:
    Her skin is as white as leprosy,

YOUNG MARINER:
    The nightmare Life-in-Death is she,
    Who thicks man's blood with cold.

ANCIENT MARINER:
    The naked hulk alongside came,
    And the twain were casting dice;

Death throws dice six times, pointing to a MARINER
*after each throw, save the sixth. The shaking of the dice
is like a death-rattle.*

WOMAN:
    The game is done! I've won, I've won!

ANCIENT MARINER:
    And then she whistles thrice.

Three strange whistling sounds which pain the
MARINER'S *ears.*

ANCIENT MARINER:
    The Sun's rim dips; the stars rush out:
    At one stride comes the dark;
    With far-heard whisper, o'er the sea,
    Off shot the spectre-bark.

The boat slides off in a burst of blinding white light.

    We listened and looked sideways up!

Fear at my heart, as at a cup,
My life-blood seemed to sip!
The stars were dim, and thick the night.
The steersman's face by his lamp gleamed white;
From the sails the dew did drip –
Till clomb above the eastern bar
The hornéd Moon, with one bright star
Within the nether tip.

One after one, by the star-dogged Moon,
Too quick for groan or sigh,
Each turned his face with a ghastly pang,
And cursed me with his eye.

Four times fifty living men,
And I heard nor sigh nor groan,
With heavy thump, a lifeless lump,
They dropped down one by one.

DEATH *removes souls symbolically. An effect must be
found for the souls to fly up.*

The souls did from their bodies fly –
They fled to bliss or woe!
And every soul it passed me by,
Like the whizz of my cross bow!

*Break back to present, dancing, music etc. A repeat of
the ghostly celebration. Up stage centre where boat was
seen,* WEDDING-GUEST *appears.*

WEDDING-GUEST:
I fear thee, ancient Mariner!
I fear thy skinny hand!
And thou art long, and lank, and brown,
As is the ribbed sea-sand.

I fear thee and thy glittering eye,
And thy skinny hand, so brown –

ANCIENT MARINER:
> Fear not, fear not, thou Wedding-Guest!
> This body dropt not down.

YOUNG MARINER:
> Alone, alone,

ANCIENT MARINER:
>   All, all alone,
> Alone on a wide wide sea!
> And never a saint took pity on
> My soul in agony.
>
> The many men, so beautiful!
> And they all dead did lie:
> And a thousand thousand slimy things
> Lived on; and so did I.

Sound of music and revelry etc. wells up. The surreal effect becomes the present and the celebration continues at normal pace on into the interval. MARINER *stays stage centre.*

Dim pre-set. Fade to spot on ANCIENT MARINER. *Others exit. Houselights.*

INTERVAL

PART TWO

Music from off-stage. The ship is as before. The houselights fade. The cast re-assembles. The YOUNG MARINER *is up stage of the mast. The* ANCIENT MARINER *is down stage. It is night and moonlight.*

ANCIENT MARINER:
>   All, all alone,
> Alone on a wide wide sea!
> And never a saint took pity on
> My soul in agony.
>
> The many men, so beautiful!
> And they all dead did lie:
> And a thousand thousand slimy things
> Lived on; and so did I.

The music fades.

YOUNG MARINER:
> I looked upon the rotting sea,
> And drew my eyes away;

YOUNG MARINER:
> I looked upon the rotting deck,
> And there the dead men lay.
>
> I closed my lids, and kept them close,
> And the balls like pulses beat;
> From the sky and the sea, and the sea and the sky
> Lay like a load on my weary eye,
> And the dead were at my feet.

VOICE OVER:
> A thousand thousand slimy things
> Lived on; and so did I.

ANCIENT MARINER:

> The moving Moon went up the sky,
> And nowhere did abide:
> Softly she was going up,
> And a star or two beside –
>
> But where the ship's huge shadow lay,
> The charmed water burnt alway
> A still and awful red.

*Images are created stage left, right and centre, with
ribbons and ropes whirled round as before.*

YOUNG MARINER:

> Beyond the shadow of the ship,
> I watched the water-snakes:
> They moved in tracks of shining white,
> And when they reared, the elfish light
> Fell off in hoary flakes.
>
> Within the shadow of the ship
> I watched their rich attire:
> Blue, glossy green, and velvet black,
> They coiled and swam; and every track
> Was a flash of golden fire.

Finish the ribbons.

ANCIENT MARINER:

> O happy living things! No tongue
> Their beauty might declare:
> A spring of love gushed from my heart,
> And I blessed them unaware:

YOUNG MARINER:

> The self-same moment I could pray;
> And from my neck so free
> The Albatross fell off, and sank
> Like lead into the sea.

YOUNG MARINER *lowers Albatross slowly out of sight.*

ANCIENT MARINER:

> Oh sleep! It is a gentle thing,
> Beloved from pole to pole!
> To Mary Queen the praise be given!
> She sent the gentle sleep from Heaven,
> That slid into my soul.

YOUNG MARINER *curls up slowly at feet of* ANCIENT MARINER. *Sleeps. Rain effect.*

> The salty buckets on the deck,
> That had so long remained,
> I dreamt that they were filled with dew;
> And when I awoke, it rained.

> My lips were wet, my throat was cold,
> My garments all were dank;
> Sure I had drunken in my dreams,
> And still my body drank.

YOUNG MARINER *begins to move.*

> I moved, and could not feel my limbs:
> I was so light – almost
> I thought that I had died in sleep,
> And was a blessèd ghost.

Wind effect.

> And soon I heard a roaring wind:
> It did not come annear;
> But with its sound it shook the sails,
> That were so thin and sere.

Sails are shaken. Images are created by whirling ribbons and ropes. Wind builds up through scene. Lightning flashes and dancing lights.

> The upper air burst into life!

And a hundred fire-flags sheen,
To and fro they were hurried about!
And to and fro, and in and out,
The wan stars danced between.

YOUNG MARINER *works the ropes.*

And the coming wind did roar more loud,
And the sails did sigh like sedge;
And the rain poured down from one black cloud;
The Moon was at its edge.

YOUNG MARINER:
The loud wind never reached the ship,

Wind fades and the sails shake.

Yet now the ship moves on!
Beneath the lightning and the Moon
The dead men gave a groan.

ANCIENT MARINER:
They groaned, they stirred, they all uprose,
Nor spake, nor moved their eyes;
It had been strange, even in a dream,
To have seen those dead men rise.

The helmsmen steered, the ship moved on;
Yet never a breeze up-blew!
The mariners all 'gan work the ropes,
Where they were wont to do:
They raised their limbs like lifeless tools –
We were a ghastly crew.

The body of my brother's son
Stood by me, knee to knee:
The body and I pulled at one rope,
But he said nought to me.

He toiled where he was wont to do

Without respite or rest.
'Twas not those souls that fled in pain,
Which to their corses came again,
But a troop of spirits blest:

For when it dawned – they dropped their arms,
And clustered round the mast;

The dead MARINERS *follow the directions of the poem.*
They end up clustered round the mast. They hum an
antiphonal chorus of Hymn, intermingled with other
sounds on tape.

YOUNG MARINER:
Sweet sounds rose slowly through their mouths,
And from their bodies passed.

Around, around, flew each sweet sound,
Then darted to the Sun;
Slowly the sounds came back again,
Now mixed, now one by one.

And now 'twas like all instruments,
Now like a lonely flute;
And now it is an angel's song,
That makes the Heavens be mute.

Sounds – cut out. Lights change. Strange sound of
sails.

It ceased; yet still the sails made on
A pleasant noise till noon,
A noise like of a hidden brook
In the leafy month of June,
That to the sleeping woods all night
Singeth a quiet tune.

ANCIENT MARINER:
Till noon we quietly sailed on,
Yet never a breeze did breathe:

Slowly and smoothly went the ship,
Moved onward from beneath.

Under the keel nine fathom deep,
From the land of mist and snow,
The spirit slid: and it was he
That made the ship to go.
The sails at noon left off their tune,
And the ship stood still also.

Silence.

The Sun, right up above the mast,
Had fixed her to the ocean:
But in a minute she 'gan stir,
With a short uneasy motion –

YOUNG MARINER:
Backwards and forwards half her length,
With a short uneasy motion.

SAILORS *work ropes, ladders, and sail, backwards and
forwards, more and more violently. The* YOUNG
MARINER *is thrown around from rigging to rigging.*

Then like a pawing horse let go,
She made a sudden bound:

ANCIENT MARINER:
It flung the blood into my head,
And I fell down in a swound.

*Thunder crash and lightning flash. A single spot only
on* ANCIENT MARINER.

How long in that same fit I lay,
I have not to declare;
But ere my living life returned,
I heard, and in my soul discerned
Two voices in the air.

*Two single spots light up two disembodied heads,
suspended in harnesses left and right, or somehow
appearing to float in space. The* YOUNG MARINER's
*body is lifted high in the air by the sailors and is held
throughout the voices with a light on it.*

VOICE 1:

> Is it he? Is this the man?
> By Him who died on cross,
> With his cruel bow he laid full low
> The harmless Albatross.
>
> The spirit who bideth by himself
> In the land of mist and snow,
> He loved the bird that loved the man
> Who shot him with his bow.

ANCIENT MARINER:

> The other was a softer voice,
> As soft as honey-dew:

VOICE 2:

> The man hath penance done,
> And penance more will do.

VOICE 1:

> But tell me, tell me! Speak again,
> Thy soft response renewing –
> What makes that ship drive on so fast?
> What is the ocean doing?

VOICE 2:

> Still as a slave before his lord,
> The ocean hath no blast;
> His great bright eye most silently
> Up to the Moon is cast –
>
> If he may know which way to go;
> For she guides him smooth or grim.

See, brother, see! how graciously
She looketh down on him.

VOICE 1:

But why drives on that ship so fast,
Without or wave or wind?

VOICE 2:

The air is cut away before,
And closes from behind.

Fly, brother, fly! more high, more high!
Or we shall be belated:

VOICE 1:

For slow and slow that ship will go,
When the Mariner's trance is abated.

Fade lights down to spot on ANCIENT MARINER.
SAILORS *move into group up stage.*

ANCIENT MARINER:

I woke, and we were sailing on
As in a gentle weather:
'Twas night, calm night, the Moon was high;
The dead men stood together.

Lights up on group. The YOUNG MARINER *is
transfixed on rigging. The action follows the direction
of the poem.*

All stood together on the deck,
For a charnel-dungeon fitter:
All fixed on me their stony eyes,
That in the Moon did glitter.

The pang, the curse, with which they died,
Had never passed away:
I could not draw my eyes from theirs,
Nor turn them up to pray.

YOUNG MARINER *snaps his head away. Blackout. The*
SAILORS *exit. Re-establish moonlight.*

> And now this spell was snapt; once more
> I viewed the ocean green,
> And looked far forth, yet little saw
> Of what had else been seen –

A breeze arises.

> But soon there breathed a wind on me,
> Nor sound nor motion made:
> Its path was not upon the sea
> In ripple or in shape.

> Swiftly, swiftly flew the ship,
> Yet she sailed softly too:
> Sweetly, sweetly blew the breeze –
> On me alone it blew.

*The image of the shoreline is silhouetted on the sail, and
the warning bell is heard. The* YOUNG MARINER
climbs the rigging to look out.

YOUNG MARINER:
> Oh! dream of joy! is this indeed
> The light-house top I see?
> Is this the hill? Is this the kirk?
> Is this mine own countree?

ANCIENT MARINER:
> The harbour-bay was clear as glass,
> So smoothly it was strewn!
> And on the bay the moonlight lay,
> And the shadow of the Moon.

> And the bay was white with silent light,
> Till rising from the same,
> Full many shapes, that shadows were,

In crimson colours came.

Red ribbons rise from the floor stage left and right. The deck is bathed in blood red light.

A little distance from the prow
Those crimson shadows were:
I turned my eyes upon the deck –

The ribbons cease

YOUNG MARINER:
Oh, Christ! What see I there!

ANCIENT MARINER:
Each corse lay flat, lifeless and flat.

YOUNG MARINER:
Now, by the holy rood!

ANCIENT MARINER:
A man all light, a seraph-man,
On every corse there stood.

The MARINERS, *clad in white silk costumes, stand up stage in a top light. They slowly raise their right arms.*

This seraph-band, each waved his hand,
No voice did they impart –
No voice; but oh! the silence sank
Like music on my heart.

SERAPHS/MARINERS *slowly fade and exit. The sound of oars and ringing is heard.*

But soon I heard the dash of oars,
I heard the Pilot's cheer;
My head was turned perforce away,
And I saw a boat appear.

Up stage centre the ribbed ghost boat re-fitted trucks forward from out of the dark.

The Pilot and the Pilot's boy,
I heard them coming fast:

YOUNG MARINER:
Dear Lord in Heaven!

ANCIENT MARINER:
It was a joy
The dead men could not blast.

Hymn.

I saw a third – I heard his voice:

YOUNG MARINER:
It is the Hermit good!
He singeth loud his godly hymns
That he makes in the wood.
He'll shrieve my soul, he'll wash away
The Albatross's blood.

ANCIENT MARINER:
The skiff-boat neared: I heard them talk,

PILOT:
Why, this is strange, I trow!
Where are those lights so many and fair,
That signal made but now?

HERMIT:
Strange, by my faith!
And they answered not our cheer!
The planks look warped! and see those sails,
How thin they are and sere!
I never saw aught like to them,
Unless perchance it were
Brown skeletons of leaves that lag
My forest-brook along.

PILOT:
Dear Lord! It hath a fiendish look.

HERMIT:
    I am a-feared – push on, push on!

ANCIENT MARINER:
    The boat came closer to the ship,
    But I nor spake nor stirred;
    The boat came close beneath the ship,
    And straight a sound was heard.

Thunder. Lightning.

    Under the water it rumbled on,
    Still louder and more dread:

*The sailors run on. Ropes, ladders, rigging are all
hauled up or let down. The effect is to leave as empty a
space as possible.*

    It reached the ship, it split the bay;
    The ship went down like lead.

*Loud thunder crack and lightning. The body of the
YOUNG MARINER is left lying on the capstan with a
lighting water-ripple effect on him.*

    Stunned by that loud and dreadful sound,
    Which sky and ocean smote,
    Like one that hath been seven days drowned
    My body lay afloat;

*Lights fade, sounds gradually fade. YOUNG MARINER
gets into boat in darkness. Lights up on him, head
dangling backwards out of boat.*

    But swift as dreams, myself I found
    Within the Pilot's boat.

    Upon the whirl, where sank the ship,
    The boat spun round and round;
    And all was still, save that the hill
    Was telling of the sound.

I moved my lips – the Pilot shrieked
And fell down in a fit;
The holy Hermit raised his eyes,
And prayed where he did sit.

I took the oars: the Pilot's boy,
Who now doth crazy go,
Laughed loud and long, and all the while
His eyes went to and fro.

BOY:

Ha! Ha! Oh me, full plain I see
The Devil knows how to row.

The boat exits slowly up stage into darkness with the
YOUNG MARINER *rowing frenetically. Then out of the*
dark the YOUNG MARINER *comes forward, followed*
by the HERMIT.

ANCIENT MARINER:

And now, all in my own countree,
I stood on the firm land!
The Hermit stepped forth from the boat,
And scarcely he could stand.

YOUNG MARINER:

O shrieve me, shrieve me, holy man!

ANCIENT MARINER:

The Hermit crossed his brow.

HERMIT:

Say quick, I bid thee say –
What manner of man art thou?

ANCIENT MARINER:

Forthwith this frame of mine was wrenched
With a woeful agony,
Which forced me to begin my tale;
And then it left me free.

YOUNG MARINER:
> There was a ship . . .

Fade out on scene. The exit.

ANCIENT MARINER:
> Since then, at an uncertain hour,
> That agony returns:
> And till my ghastly tale is told
> This heart within me burns.

Moves to audience.

> I pass, like night, from land to land;
> I have strange power of speech;
> The moment that his face I see

Searches out faces in the audience.

> I know the man that must hear me:
> To him my tale I teach.

Lights change. Back to present. The WEDDING-
GUESTS *enter up stage. Music.*

WEDDING-GUEST:
> What loud uproar bursts from that door!
> The wedding-guests are there:
> And in the garden-bower the bride
> And bride-maids singing are:
> And hark the little vesper bell,
> Which biddeth me to prayer!

ANCIENT MARINER:
> O Wedding-Guest! This soul hath been
> Alone on a wide wide sea:
> So lonely 'twas, that God himself
> Scarce seemed there to be.

> Farewell, farewell! but this I tell
> To thee, thou Wedding-Guest!

He prayeth best, who loveth best
All things both great and small;
For the dear God who loveth us,
He made and loveth all.

Celebration music and Morris Dance. The ANCIENT
MARINER *leaves the* WEDDING-GUEST *on his own and
stands watching the dancers.*

At the end of dance fade to spot on WEDDING-GUEST
and ANCIENT MARINER. *Sound of wind and sea
shanty in distance.* ANCIENT MARINER *is silhouetted
against the mast up stage. The dancers have gone. Fade
to blackout.*

THE END